SEASONS OF CHANGE

Seasons
of Change

—

Wild Poems

DIANA RADOVAN

OUTPOST PRESS
ABIQUIU, NEW MEXICO

OUTPOST PRESS

© 2025 TEXT BY DIANA RADOVAN

Published in 2025 by Outpost Press
Cover Design and Interior Design by Connor Wolfe
TRADE PAPERBACK 978-1-965320-48-8

10 9 8 7 6 5 4 3 2 1

Look for our titles in paperback, ebook, and audiobook wherever books are sold.
Wholesale offerings for retailers available through Ingram.

Outpost Press is committed to ecological stewardship.
We greatly value the natural environment and invest in conservation.

CONTENTS

FALL – LOSS

WINTER – LONGING

SPRING — LOVE

ACKNOWLEDGMENTS

A shorter, earlier version of this collection, the 2021 poetry chapbook *Seasons of Change*, was commended among 320 entries in the *2021 Fool for Poetry Chapbook Competition* (judged by Patrick Cotter). At the time of manuscript submission/publication, almost half of the poems included here (sometimes as earlier, slightly different versions) have previously won distinctions, have been published or have been accepted for publication elsewhere:

"If You Want to Know Me" by *Wax Poetry and Art*, as a second-place winner in the *First Calgary International Poetry Contest* with subsequent inclusion in *World's Best Poems Volume I*

"Bear Wings" by *Midway Journal*, as a finalist in the *Action, Words* contest

"I Live In Words" and "Wolf" by *Wild Roof Journal*

"Tracks," "Disconnection," "Skin," "Going Home," and "Mother Sells Water from the Fountain" by *Headline Poetry and Press*

"Dreams of Fog" and "Maybe It Is Not Too Late" by *ARC Journal*

"Willow" by *Dog-Ear*

"Silence" by *Poetry Breakfast*

"Sound" by *The Orchards Poetry Journal*

"Growth" by *The Festival of Poetry*

"Earth Mother" and "Body" by *Arcana Munich - Stories*

"Winter" by *Litro Magazine US*

Romanian versions of "*Winter*" and "*Hibernation*"
by *O mie de semne*

"Beyond Comprehension" by *The Purposeful Mayonnaise*
Story was written as part of the *peetmenotleave challenge*
and included in my hybrid memoir *Our Voices* (Troubador
Publishing, 2022)
The German version of "Cafeneaua Verde" has been published
in the *2024 Stafette Anthology*

I would like to thank my poetry mentors, in no particular order:
Brigid Yuknavitch, Jena Schwartz, Alina Ștefănescu, Jose Hernandez
Diaz, Jessica J. Lee, Silvia Grădinaru, and Lena Chilari for creating
the experimental, permissive, and inclusive online spaces where
most of the first drafts of these poems were written, critiqued, and
polished. Additionally, fellow poets and writers Claudia Tănăsescu,
Sylvia Clare, Pauline Herbst, Tessa Jacobs, Ella Voss, Nutan Jäger, and
Arnold Schlachter have provided insightful feedback on my poetry
and helped improve either individual poems in this volume or the
collection as a whole.

PROLOGUE:
IF YOU WANT TO KNOW ME

if you want to know me, don't ask me where I come from.
don't ask me whether my home country is nothing but black
all over my body. don't ask me questions about my endless scars.

don't ask me about the nights under a violet fog in which you were
watching the stars looking for complementary orange, and I the cold
ground, unable to face the half-dead bodies dangling like hammocks
underneath a sky where nobody wanted to die.

your hope now carries the colors red, white, and blue, but mine is
covered in dust particles and names of people I can no longer meet
or trust. underneath all that, it is still a pure, wild shade of green. the
color of hope should not be split into two.

ask me about my childhood dreams and I'll ship them to you, ask
me how many of them came true, please, don't give me labels,
don't call me names, don't split *Me* from *You*.

and if you'd ask me all that, I'd tell you that only one came true.
and that is more than some people have in one hundred trips
around the sun, moon, and stars.

the sun was yellow, then indigo. we couldn't tell pirates from mermaids,
riding the waves, faces pressed into one another.
even at the shore, the waves kept moving, slower, faster.

if you want to know me, sit with me inside this human temple
I've built for you out of the scar tissue of all our ancestors,
passed from generation to generation into all of *Me* and all of *You*.

sit with me and tell me stories in rediscovered or invented languages,
until your tears find shelter inside my chest and my right ventricle finds
a land of kisses around your temples. until our hearts become rainbows
that melt into one another as only homes can do.

Summer

—

Lust

AND IF I TOLD YOU

And if I told you that I crave to find shelter inside your tired body,
cover myself in scar tissue inside your rib cage,
learn the history of your cells, all the times they divided and died,

go back with you in time, into your childhood,
dream the dreams you dreamed
inside your mother's womb
when you didn't even know that's what they were,

and if I told you that I crave to be there on the day
that your mother and father first talked about conceiving you,
identify all the genes that were transferred
from generation to generation, from them into you,

place them under a microscope and tag them
with fluorescent markers,
discover all the mutations
that make your body you,

and if I told you that this is the only way I can imagine
to enter your body like a man,
and stay there forever a part of you,
if that's what I'd choose to be,

and if I told you that I crave to touch your dreams
the way you touch my skin, would you tell me:

Don't you know that wild flowers belong on fields
and it isn't up to you to tell the poppy from its seed?

Would you think that I am crazy or that I love you
despite my desire to own you,
to never see you free of me,
to never be set free?

ARE YOU THE OCEAN?

Water takes the place of your bones inside me,
    In waves that fill me only to leave, then return.

    Your body is like water, subsiding, riding the sunset,
        Meeting the sky at the line of the horizon.

            May I be both your sunshine and your clouds?
            Or should I anchor you to my shore?

            Waiting for centuries for you to cut
            Your path through me.

        Craving corrosion and turning sand into stone,
    Or was it the other way around?

    Your oceans lay bare before me,
Inviting me to drown.

GOING HOME

In the park where human-sized gods
Are set above us in white marble,
A snail leads the way, not hiding.
Trees carry memories of home.

It is here that I seek wildness,
Beyond the trimmed bushes, into the forest.
Here, the path seems to vanish
And so does time.

I've walked this land many times, on dry leaves or wet embraces.
The tree with snake-like scales is always there.
There are no other trees like it here,
In the city forest.

I have seen some in the mountains.
Five of them, and counting.
Near the waterfalls, in the darkness,
Sharing embraces that don't belong.

SOUND

Water fills the silence with sound—
In the caves of my being there is still room for air.
Birds travel faster than meaning.
Today, longing is a burning tree.

My words turn into music, into dreaming –
Your mouth is an open receptacle.
We draw the lines of our lust
Like snakes in the sand.

Bones crack under the rotating sun,
Night slowly covers your shoulders.
We do not need stars to feel warm—
Our bodies are beating hearts.

FULL CIRCLE

I am not a room for your joys and sorrows,
Not a carpet you can take to bed.
I am the motion of the ocean inside you,
Spilling its vastness over your head.
I am my own disaster, my own volcano and spring.
There is no such thing as everafter,
When squares are triangles
And circles are dead.

CROSSINGS

All crossings are a part
of your heart
spiraling back
to nature.

LIFE

Life—
series of moments,
fleeting whispers,
rays of sun.

Everything and nothing—
a heart beat hanging
on walls
with eyes.

ROOM

There has to be more room
For yellow dances around the moon.
There has to be more yellow,
More dancing, more moon.
And if there isn't, we have to make it.
The magic, the music, the room.

GATES

Gates will tell you a thousand stories
If you stand still and listen
To the past whisper
And coming alive.

WOLF

A wolf visits my dreams
and tells me about the crossing
to the other world,
one of joy but also of constant hunger.

On the moon it doesn't matter
if I am or not the wolf—
we are not enemies
and we are not water.

The wolf in my dreams
is not in the forest
but in my room.
I am a little girl on a chair.

Later I write about the girl
who lives in the hollow of a tree
and is the healer of the forest,
the girl who runs with the wolves.

The girl becomes the High Priestess
and when all wolves die
hunted down by evil humans
she creates a new forest.

MOTHER SELLS WATER FROM THE FOUNTAIN

Mother sells water from the fountain, 20 *bani* a cup.

There's a heat wave in this city,

There's thirst and hunger in this country.

On some days, the hunger can still be fought.

There are things in this city, in this country,

Things not to be talked about,

Family members held silent behind bars.

Books my child-mother reads on her birthday with her friend S.,

whose father is also not to be talked about.

Dissidents! Criminals! Traitors of their country!

The cherry flowers are in full bloom,

There is still unpoisoned water in the fountain

And books to be passed around.

Mother sells water from the fountain, 20 *bani* a cup.

EARTH MOTHER

I am a mother and a wife. I am a writer and a woman. I am someone who wakes up in the mountains, before everyone else. Not to clean the house, not to write, not to prepare breakfast, but to breathe in the wet morning air.

To wander the streets on my own, to cross that bridge, into the forest, where waterfalls just are and just flow, into a river, not a lake. To climb that steep mountain path and find those trees that only belong in the forest and would always look lost in the city. To dig my hands deep into the earth—the earth that is wet, but not dirty, and so full of yet unexplored life.

I am a mother and a wife, and if I do not return home right now, if I linger in the forest just a little longer, or a lot, and if my daughter and my son are no longer sleeping, my husband will be there to take care of them. And if my daughter and my son wouldn't be twins, they would still be who they are—themselves, not our mirror reflections.

I am a woman and I am my own house. My words are not broken and they are always heard and trusted. I am not my genes. Each one of us living here is a house of his or her own making. Inside the house, there are many rooms. Each room feels like a mother's womb, but the doors are always open, to enter and exit.

TRACKS

Life and death, two parallel lines.
In between you—
This body you cannot escape.

Fall

—

Loss

THIS BABY

This baby could be ours, here,
on a bed of branches.
This baby could have parents.
This baby could get shelter.
If only, if only.
This baby cannot see them.
They left behind just hunger;
no milk, no breast, no bedsheets.
Only the moon can see him,
only the sun can burn him.
This baby could hear gunshots,
and marching boots and whistles.
Its eyes are gone in darkness,
the raven claws have shaped them.
This baby could grow feathers,
this baby could be breastfed.
No boat will take this baby,
no man will hear its laughter.
Its mother's womb forsook it
before it breathed and crumbled.
Forgotten is this baby.
It never was, this baby.
It never knew life's meaning,
no breast, no milk, no laughter.
The boat will take them further.
If only, if only.

JOY

Joy can be soft, stern, or in colors,
It can hide in raindrops, it can blow your mind.

A kiss under the morning sun,
The rain, forgotten.

A place that grows inside you
Instead of falling deep into the ocean.

Carrying the ruins of a smile, of hands you used to touch,
Of eyes you used to love.

WE ARE LOVERS

We find reasons to hate
Just like we find reasons to love.
Love is the word we use
When mating silently in the dark
Inside sealed boxes we selfishly call *homes,*
Inside sealed safeties we proudly call
The-joy-of-marriage and
Our-deep-love-for-one-another.

Except that there are cracks
Building up in our tall white walls.
Yellow flowers growing wild
In our overtrimmed gardens.
Dreams that cannot escape
Because they're too closely sealed
By our *hold-me-tight-please*
Love-hate of one another.

CITY OF MY CHILDHOOD

City of my childhood,
You're a forgotten body
I can no longer own.
I remain a passenger through you,
Who can never return.

THE SOUND OF SILENCE IS RED

Nobody will ever love me became a mantra, a circle of grief.

My mother's voice was crimson. I screamed like a wild cat.

Stars were splashed across the ceiling. We lived on Romulus Street.

Cramps took the place of my legs. I continued screaming, half-asleep.

We do not know our endings or beginnings.

Nobody will ever love me became a mantra, a circle of grief.

NIHILISM

I went on a dinner date with Emil Cioran. Neither of us mentioned
the word *nihilism*. Neither of us mentioned his death, nor the fact
that he had spent his entire life moving towards it. We didn't talk
about his childhood, the lost paradise of his native village, how he'd
play football with the skulls at the cemetery. We ordered wine at
candle light. I was old, already older than him. We talked about
the weather, *it rains a lot in Paris*, he said. We let the rain cover
our plates. We did not leave, the night fell and its heavy shoulders
became ours. Our dinner never ended, the nothingness he felt
seeped into my veins.

MOMENT

Country music, a café at the North Atlantic,
Alcohol-free beer, art on walls
In colors of the rainbow and my hair –

Too straight to be mine.
It's from the AC on the plane,
It happens every time.

I feel like I've turned
Into a river, a forest, an ocean –
Somebody else's dream, not mine.

THIS IS, THESE ARE

These are my arms—longer than most,
with ears instead of fingers, tree branches turned to stone,
without water or sun, all I can do is
wait-hope-cry-fly-wait-hope-cry-fly.

This is my mouth—an open wound
with words spilling out, spilling out, spilling out,
one word after another, like legs pounding
on empty roads that nobody else seems to know.

This is my breath—catch it if you can,
but expect a wind, it will not stop,
expect to be blown apart, expect nothing but the unexpected,
for I do know what kind of wind I am.

These are my eyes—seeing you seeing me,
making the world whole,
then tearing it to pieces,
then making it whole, then tearing it to pieces.

This is my question—where shall we begin?
We tell stories that never end,
always start. I want to be more than this stillness, this motion,
this longing, this crying, this, always in my bones, heaviness, then
flying,
not knowing where to go or why, why are we always apart.

A part of *apart*—missing the point,
there are no lines before us to climb all the way to the sky.
This is us unfailing, unending, undoing, unwanting,
back into the future of all the stars.

GIANT

My body is a sleeping mountain,
A giant not be awakened,
Not before the rising sun.

Stars rise above it
But nobody can see them—
A rainbow would mean the giant woke up.

My pockets of earth
Hide stories of tomorrow,
Untold before the soil has settled.

Rocks take the place of my shoulders.
Imagine an earthquake, please,
Or the lava of a dying volcano.

Wings stay unimaginable—
All I have is this one morning
Before the rising sun.

GROWTH

Inside the ivory tower
We sit and wait for a prince
To come and cut
The story short
Or maybe just our hair
While our hands grow scissors.

WILLOW

The willow danced, her moves did not care about the crowd, her hands drew circles in the air, like caterpillars falling down from apples, they crossed over unseen faces, caressing their every pore, she twirled embracing human bodies only she could see, and the room was dark, and still, and the light was red, in the Theater-Podium bar, and only the little black cat in the corner watched and whispered through her purrs to the trees in the forest in which she thought she was, she said, look, although there is no river, and no human to cry next to her, here's a willow with a female face, with long dark-red hair that falls onto stones like branches, a woman who forgot to dream but became a dream herself, forsaken by male touch and baby hugs, look, the cat said, there's a woman almost taking off and leaving the ground, rooting her hands deep into the clouds. But the cat was just a cat, and the forest did not listen, because there was no forest, and there was no ground, and the music stopped, and the willow was now asleep, with a little black blind kitten curled up at her feet, and the next performance, and the audience, they were nowhere to be found, and the willow's voice was dreaming of a time when she would sing each night, it was either opera or jazz, and the willow was young and voluptuous back then, she was nothing like a willow at all, and the willow's voice fell asleep too, deep in her stomach, away from human sounds, behind the curtains, and never again was it to be found.

DISCONNECTION

Layers of scar tissue unfold under the microscope.

It is here that I seek beauty,

In the darkness.

Images need magnifying

To bring out the truth.

We carry many truths within our bodies.

Animals naturally shake to release trauma.

Sometimes, we forget.

Our bodies remember

And our brains try to hold on.

Disconnections flutter.

Lesions in our white matter

Affect our perception of time.

The past becomes tomorrow.

A dead mother becomes a presence.

IRIS

Stillness
Like an eye
That can dance
But hasn't yet learned
To see.

Winter

—

Longing

SILENCE

Mother was swallowed by sharks.
First her hands, then her mouth, then her hair.
Now all mother's words are being carried on water,
While mother is silent, like a fish.

HIBERNATION

We'd go to bed at 6 pm on the days
you now call *The Romanian Revolution.*
At least, I would, and the world would then stop turning for me.
Except in my dreams, or, shall I say, nightmares.
The gunshots would sometimes wake me up at night.
But mostly, the gunshots took the place of our voices at daytime.
On the TV, only one voice would rise
above all others until just a week ago.
My voice, so small under that of my parents.
My mother's voice, so small under that of my father.
My grandmother, so small.
I, a child. A child wearing a yellow belt.
A little commander, too afraid to use her voice.
Dreaming that I have lost my parents.
Dreaming that our house has been turned
into a carpet of holes left by bullets.
Even in my dreams, the walls were barely standing.
The microphones in the walls were there, *the ears*
that *had been pressed to the ground.*
We'd go to bed at 6 pm on the days
you now call *The Romanian Revolution.*

WINTER

In winter, my mother would take me sledding.
She would be my horse.
In winter, everything was white and calm, until it wasn't.
In winter, my grandmother would cook and roast
And prepare a separate meal for each of us:
my aunt, my cousin, my uncle, and me.
In winter, my grandmother would die.
In winter, my mother would turn her back to us
and sleep, sleep, sleep.
In winter, I would celebrate Christmas alone with my father.
My mother though, she was supposedly still alive.
We would sometimes still gather around the kitchen table—
my father, my mother, and I.
In winter, I would be alone sometimes.
In winter, I would forget what home tastes like.
In winter, the German cabbage leaves would not bend
like the Romanian ones.
In Germany, we would complain and long for
the *sarmale* of our childhood.
In winter, I would forget my name.
I would reinvent myself.
I would get abandoned by the man I once followed.
I would move, again and again.

I would find silence, and peace, in the village
that was never really mine.
In the surrounding hills that echoed my name,
Day after day, voice after voice, one tree after another.
In winter, I would sometimes turn and unturn into my mother.

DREAMS OF FOG

Your ego craves things. It longs to settle down. It craves to go places. Walk new paths, meet new people, kind, warmer, more intelligent, more open-minded, more peaceful people. It wants to put them all into tiny drawers and take them out only when it feels like it, but no, they have minds and egos of their own, they meet up in cafés and dancing halls and bedrooms, they intertwine their bodies in beds that were once yours, in places that were once *home*.

It's morning, 7 a.m. The sliced mountains are topped with snow. He brushes his beard against your face, scratching the surface of your skin. You love the pain and the heaviness of his warm, tobacco-filled breath, so close to your lips that always miss him. He says that life is hard, that people hurt, that he would have never thought two people could ever inflict so much pain upon each other *out of love*. If he means his ex-wife, you, or any of his other women, you don't know. He is eaten up by years, wind, thoughts, and cancer cells. He is sour and raw. His daughter looks at you with big eyes and little curls, soft like daffodil petals. You stroke her head with broken hand gestures, like an interrupted thread.

You are an interrupted thread.

This moment stays in your mind for years, like a family photo, not your family, but your moment, when you told yourself that we people are OK as we are, with all the luggage and sadness that we give one another like a gift, even when we do not mean to.

We are all interrupted threads.

One moment of thousands of moments was not enough to please an ego as big as yours. You tried to make your ego small under watchful eyes and arms, but it couldn't keep a low profile for too long, and missed being I.

You wake up on a flat field. Snow and dreams are falling upon you, dancing in thin contours under a vertical sky of fog. Two trees are growing as one around a wooden cross.

It could be morning, there could be light.

BEAR WINGS

Berries and coffins   this is how I find you
The sugar and the death   here at once

Lift me up   you say but I cannot listen
Lift yourself up   my body yells

Tonight we drift   into nothingness
Stars will not touch   either of us

Sand travels fast   kiss hold hands
Trespass the orange light   across oceans

What's left   when the winds pass   the dirt
Yellow snow   from the window   I watch it

What if   your body was a sunset
turning into comets   no berries no coffins

ALMOST SUNRISE

Stars in the morning—
You'd see them too if only
You stopped
Looking for the sun.

HEART

The heart is just a muscle,
He said.
But I went on
Carving hearts
Out of rainbows,
Turning them
Into cotton candy clouds
And gifting them,
To strangers.

OUR BODIES ARE 70% WATER

It started with a thunderstorm, a word I didn't know.
It started with an aunt, *my* aunt, not letting go of my hand.
We used towels in our window frames
as the street was swallowed by rain.
Later, I drowned instead of learning how to swim.
Our bodies are 70% water, like our earth.
So many lakes built on sunk villages!
Legends keep coming alive there.
Water and earth monsters meet at the bottom.
Rivers continue to flow into one another,
into the sea that is not black.
I take my right hand into my left hand and,
step by step, drift into the snow.
Tears gather in the corner of my eyes and turn into ice.

Tears gather in the corner of my eyes and turn into ice.
I take my right hand into my left hand and,
step by step, drift into the snow.
Rivers continue to flow into one another,
into the sea that is not black.
Legends keep coming alive there.
Water and earth monsters meet at the bottom
So many lakes built on sunk villages!
Our bodies are 70% water, like our earth.

Later, I drowned instead of learning how to swim.
We used towels in our window frames
as the street was swallowed by rain.
It started with an aunt, *my* aunt, not letting go of my hand.
It started with a thunderstorm, a word I didn't know.

STORY

This story isn't only mine,
My body is just the portal that carries it.
It is born from everything we kept locked
For far too long in our bodies.

It is born from the scorched earth
That was buried deep down
Under the trees in the forest,
Under the dried out water.

Lift this weight off my shoulders,
Lift this weight from inside my body,
You, wind that flows at sunset
With the ravens, into the horizon.

What remains is only a faded memory
Whispered around the fire, when night falls,
As a warning, to children by elders,
Until it becomes legend.

RAIN

Your hands aren't wrapped around my waist,
Reality doesn't fit the frames of this picture.

Your smile cannot make it all good again,
There's truth in thunder. Storms do not whisper.

Your hands are too big for my waist,
Your smile is too slender.

Droplets caress my skin through the open door,
Winter rain brings the cold back into the room.

Rain touches me better than you.
To this moment, I surrender.

LIGHT

Attainable is the light
Even when it only
Split into colors
Passes by.

STONE

Winter
Turns silence
To stone.

WALD

In the forest I am free,
Growing wildly, like a tree,
With the birds,
Towards the sky.

Spring

—

Love

THE QUESTION

I am sitting on a wooden bench at 1416 metres, drinking coffee.
Listening to ice becoming water on the rooftop
 and flowing down, down, down
At the Katrin Berggasthof above the spa town of Bad Ischl.
European Capital of Culture 2024. The mountains in one direction
Remain still in the distance, covered in snow.

Getting up here by cable car,
I see the Wildenstein ruins close to the valley,
I see smaller mountains below my resting legs
just about to meet their young grass,
Their earth still mostly raw and brown, as I keep looking down
In the milky morning light for an answer.
As I keep looking at the cut down trees,
Their roots exposed, the clear traces of human destruction
meant to create this path up.
Meanwhile the mountains look like the arched backs of giant sleepers.
They look like they'd know, like they've always known,
The answers to all our questions.

I am here, a beating heart and muscles, slowly growing white hair
Somewhere between Germany, Austria, Romania,
With memories of the Banff Centre in Alberta, Canada.

With vivid memories of my first days of writing here
In the depth of winter, with the wind seeping deeply into my bones.
The days of calling Sleepy Buffalo my magic mountain.

The days of walking into town,
of passing through the gateless cemetery,
A tourist, a temporary Calgary resident,
both feeling and not feeling at home.
Looking for *My Way* among all others,
wandering the streets that carry animal names.
Goat Street, Bear Street, Elk Street.
Streets like the origin of an ancient longing.
Streets like an Earth-Mother.

I am sitting on a wooden bench at 1416 metres, drinking coffee.
Asking myself: should I use
British or American English in this meandering essay
that keeps on pretending to be a poem?
I'm drinking coffee surrounded by small, playful children
who do not question themselves,
Their feet keep finding their way without fear
through the slushy snow up the mountain,
To the top, up, up, up, their little lungs relentlessly pumping
their souls into answers.

I keep asking myself if my womb will ever, could have ever,
Bear-bear, there-there,
Any kind of fruit.

ABOUT THE OCEAN

And perhaps it is not today
That I will tell you
About the ocean,
Because today the ocean
Is only a sea.

Only the sun,
Only a light ray.
This only
And this alone.

Only touches lit by the earth-moon,
Only mirrors lit by the oceans.
Because today the ocean
Is only a sea.

Carrying your heart beat,
Carrying your footsteps,
Out at bay, into the ocean,
Onto the mountains.

Into the snow caves,
Into the valleys,
Into the fjords,
Into the morning.

Into the moment.
Into the silence.
Into the night,
Into the light.

BRODERIE

Blooms, branches, and books,
Broderie. Untranslatable brown and red
Longing for green, a crescent heart breeding leaves
That might turn purple or blue.

BODY

You becomes *I* when you surrender,
Love becomes possible.
The limbs of that little girl
Too tall, too skinny, too shy—
Never exactly what the world expected
Grew into this possibility
That you now call existence
As walking the earth becomes tomorrow,
As remembering life and family
Becomes you.

The hawk lands in hunger
And the forest remains standing.
Look at that cliff,
The trees growing around it,
Grabbing it with all their power,
Their roots in full expansion.
Look at yourself,
There is a mirror everywhere.
The entire world echoes in heartbeats,
I, I, I, here, alive.

SKIN

I shed layers of skin like the green snake
I see in the morning grass of the castle gardens.
Inside my body lives a woman I haven't met yet. She is young,
But her soul is older than memory. Sometimes, I hear her whisper.
She does not roar.

The snake brushes against the carpet of dry leaves.
Near Neptune's fountain,
Medusa's head lies trapped in stone,
In the hands of Athena, Goddess of Wisdom and War.

I cross the bridge of branches to the other side, into the woods.
I discover the trees within myself, with everything they carry.;

Their sap is moving upwards into everything, everywhere.
I feel the sun burn on my skin.
The old woman is alive, wilder and bigger than life!
Her voice is rising inside me, a wild rose breaking through stone.

THE RIVER KNOWS

The river knows what your heart refuses to see,
The river flows among you and her and him and me.

The river knows
Where to flow,
The forest grows
Under the snow.

The mountains rise
When moonlight falls
And dreams take shape
When we let go.

The river whispers the sun to the moon,
The birds dream the dreams that their home-river flows.

MOUNTAIN-HEART

If my heart were a mountain,
It would scream for valleys,
It would live in echoes—
Meeting air, not stone.

ENCOUNTER

Earth and sky
meet and greet
brown to green
blue my heart
silence is
no longer craving
peace is language
oceans speak.

BEYOND COMPREHENSION

I was born in a family of pain. My birth was long awaited.
I was given three names instead of one.
Each carried a vessel of its own.
One was a childless goddess, protector of maidens and fertility.

I have forgotten my country of birth.
Rootless, they called me, again and again.
Where do you come from and why are you here? they would say.
The answers they gave were different from my own.

My hair grew beyond comprehension.
This became a diagnosis of its own.
If my uterus could talk, like a mouth of blood, what would it say?
I turn to words and offer them to the world.
I make and unmake the universe and its meaning.

Step by step, I keep on walking.
Solitude becomes my nest. Nature becomes my temple, my home.
I spin in cycles around my core. River after river, I am home.

LOVE

The mountains echoed—
In white, branches were shoulders.
My love, a free dove.

CAFENEAUA VERDE

I am drinking water at *Cafeneaua Verde,* long ago I'd often come here.
An art album was once flipped through, also here, by a father.
His beret remained untouched for years,
Forgotten on a coat hanger.

I close my eyes and remember. I remember us. You with beard.
Me with pigtails. On the way, on summer vacation in Herculane.
In the life of a mountain, thirty years is nothing,
The movement of an eyelid.

Near Gărâna, we'd paint waterfalls together, up on the hills.
Back then you'd tell me: *Life is more beautiful when shared.*
Other children kept gathering rocks against the water,
They were building a dam.

The life of a hyperactive woman is measured by how fast she runs
Farther and farther away from you, from herself.
I haven't been home for a very long time.
The color of your eyes I no longer know.

FRUIT-MOTHER

I was born a child
And stayed one
After discovering touch.

Tenderness is purple
With a shade of blue.
Mothers are like plums.

Strawberries are Beethoven.
Strawberries flow
Through my mother's hair.

Joy is watermelons
Cracking wide open
Under the golden sun.

MAYBE IT IS NOT TOO LATE

Maybe it is not too late to learn to let the path
come to you instead of always chasing it,
Maybe it is not too late to learn
to let the sunshine in.

The grass will keep growing tall
despite you constantly trimming it.
Mountains will still rise in echo
even as you fall asleep.

So maybe it is not too late to learn
to swim, to breathe, to float, to whisper.
You don't need to be a loud shout
to carry the signature of all things.

EPILOGUE: I LIVE IN WORDS

I live in words,
Between the pages of books
Too old to be remembered.
When the lake ran dry,
We stopped spending our holidays there.
The lake became a myth,
Words became memories.
My body has traveled.
Country after country,
Everyone asked me:
Where is home?
Beyond language, beyond borders.
In mountains, and trees,
And the depth of the ocean.
I live in woods,
In lingering in-between places
Older than language.

ABOUT THE AUTHOR

Diana Radovan from Hybrid Nature Writing Beyond Borders is the author of the hybrid memoir *Our Voices* (2022) and the essay collection *Dincolo* (2025). Romanian-born, she has mostly inhabited German and Canadian spaces in the last twenty years. Her multi-genre and cross-lingual writing—poetry, fiction, nonfiction, and hybrid forms—has been published internationally since 2004. It acts as a bridge between languages and cultures, exploring personal identity and liminality. A Forest Bathing Guide and Forest Therapy Practitioner, she also has a PhD in the Life Sciences from TU Dortmund in Germany. Currently, she is pursuing an MA in Creative Writing at Teesside University in the UK and roaming the Bavarian-Tyrolean alpine borderlands, where rock, earth, forest, air, and water feel like home.

Find out more at www.naturewriting.net.